D0537348

A TRUE BOOK™

Lyme Disease

ANN O. SQUIRE

Children's Press®
An Imprint of Scholastic Inc.

Content Consultant

Phyllis Meadows, PhD, MSN, RN

Associate Dean for Practice, Clinical Professor, Health Management and Policy

University of Michigan, Ann Arbor, Michigan

Library of Congress Cataloging-in-Publication Data

Names: Squire, Ann, author.

Title: Lyme disease / by Ann O. Squire.

Other titles: True book.

Description: New York, NY : Children's Press, an imprint of Scholastic Inc., 2016. | 2017 | Series:
A true book | Includes bibliographical references and index.

Identifiers: LCCN 2015048541| ISBN 9780531228418 (library binding) | ISBN 9780531233252 (pbk.)

Subjects: LCSH: Lyme disease—Juvenile literature. | Tick-borne diseases—Juvenile literature.

Classification: LCC RC155.5 .S68 2016 | DDC 616.9/246—dc23

LC record available at http://lccn.loc.gov/2015048541

© 2017 Scholastic Inc.

All rights reserved. Published in 2017 by Children's Press, an imprint of Scholastic Inc.
Printed in China 62

SCHOLASTIC, CHILDREN'S PRESS, A TRUE BOOK™, and associated logos are trademarks and/or registered trademarks of Scholastic Inc.

1 2 3 4 5 6 7 8 9 10 R 26 25 24 23 22 21 20 19 18 17

Front cover: Two ticks in a glass container
Back cover: A deer tick on a person's fingertip

Find the Truth!

Everything you are about to read is true *except* for one of the sentences on this page.

Which one is **TRUE**?

T or F If you are bitten by a tick, you will definitely get Lyme disease.

T or F Lyme disease is much more common in some areas of the world than others.

Find the answers in this book.

Contents

THE **BIG** TRUTH!

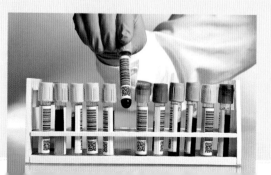

Blood tests do not always accurately show the presence of Lyme disease.

Medicine to treat Lyme disease is sometimes injected into a person's vein.

Dog ticks are a nuisance, but they don't spread Lyme disease.

CHAPTER 1

Summertime Sickness

It was the last day of summer vacation. Jackie was helping her parents and sister, Betsy, pack up clothes, toys, and everything else they had brought to the summer cottage. Jackie's parents had rented the house because it was near a beach. It also had a big yard surrounded by woods and tall grass. The kids had spent hours playing and exploring outside. They had a wonderful time!

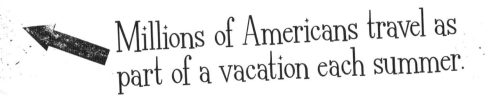

Millions of Americans travel as part of a vacation each summer.

What Can It Be?

A few days after getting home, Jackie began to feel strange. Her arms and legs ached. She had a dull headache. Sometimes she felt hot all over, and the next minute she was freezing cold. When

her mom took her temperature, she found that it was higher than normal. It seemed as though Jackie had a cold or the flu.

A high temperature can be a sign of many different illnesses.

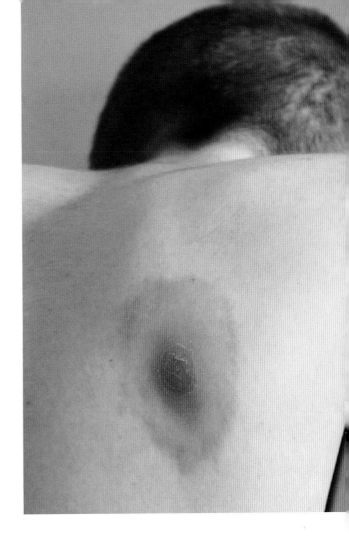

A bull's-eye rash is a telltale sign of Lyme disease.

After staying in bed the next day, Jackie was no better. Her mom was getting worried. But then she noticed something she hadn't seen before. The sleeve of Jackie's shirt was pushed up, revealing a bright-red rash on her upper arm. The rash had a red center, surrounded by two rings. It looked just like a bull's-eye. Jackie's mom called the doctor.

CHAPTER 2

Making a Diagnosis

The doctor asked about Jackie's symptoms and looked carefully at the rash. Then he asked about Jackie's summer vacation. Had she been outside a lot in wooded or grassy areas? When Jackie described the woods bordering their cottage, the doctor nodded. "I'm pretty sure you have Lyme disease," he said.

A patient's symptoms and recent experiences help doctors diagnose Lyme disease.

Deer ticks (below) are not as large as dog ticks (left).

The Trouble With Ticks

The doctor explained that people can get Lyme disease from a tick bite. Ticks are tiny **arachnids**. There are many different kinds of ticks. If you have a dog that plays outside, you may have had to remove large ticks from its coat. Dog ticks are annoying, but they are not dangerous. Lyme disease is carried by black-legged deer ticks, which are much smaller and tougher to spot.

Bloodsuckers!

Ticks are **parasites**. They feed on blood to grow and reproduce. Deer ticks feed off the blood of deer, as well as mice and other small animals. They are usually found in wooded areas or places with high grass and shrubs. The woods where Jackie and Betsy had played were the perfect habitat for deer ticks.

Deer ticks can be found in areas where deer and other animals live.

If you feel like you have a cold or the flu, think about whether you've recently been somewhere ticks could be.

An Important Clue

It was the red, bull's-eye rash and the fact that Jackie had been in a place where ticks are found that led to the doctor's **diagnosis**. Jackie's fever, chills, and body pain were simply additional evidence that Lyme disease was the problem. On their own, these symptoms were not enough to make a diagnosis of Lyme disease.

A Lucky Break

The doctor explained that Jackie was lucky the rash had developed. Not everyone who contracts Lyme disease gets a rash. Without the rash, it is much harder for a doctor to diagnose these patients correctly. Fever and muscle pain are symptoms of many common illnesses, including colds and the flu. Lyme is sometimes called the "great imitator" because it can be mistaken for so many other medical conditions.

A feeling of being tired or worn out can be a sign of Lyme disease.

You probably wouldn't notice at first if a tick bit you.

A Painless Bite

"Are you saying Jackie was bitten by a tick?" Jackie's mom asked. "We didn't see any ticks or bites."

The doctor explained that immature ticks are the ones most likely to pass on Lyme disease. At this stage, the tick is only about the size of a poppy seed. What's more, ticks have saliva that acts as an **anesthetic**. This means the person cannot feel the bite.

Testing for Lyme Disease

"Are you sure it is Lyme disease?" Jackie's mom asked. "Are there other tests you can do?"

The doctor explained that blood tests can detect **antibodies** produced by a person's **immune system** to fight Lyme disease. However, it can take weeks for antibodies to appear. Early blood tests may be negative even if a person does have Lyme. False positives (detecting Lyme disease when it's not there) are also common.

Blood tests are not a very accurate way to diagnose Lyme disease.

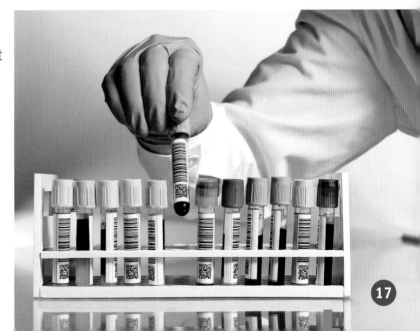

Delaying Treatment

Jackie was lucky to be diagnosed early. With treatment, she would likely make a full recovery. Because Lyme symptoms can be so confusing, it can take some people months or years to arrive at a diagnosis. Without prompt treatment, Lyme **bacteria** spread through the body. Heart problems, poor memory, numbness, and pain are some of the long-term results of untreated Lyme disease.

If Lyme disease is not treated, it can lead to chest pains and other medical problems.

The World's Oldest Lyme Patient

In 1991, two tourists hiking in the Austrian Alps discovered a human corpse frozen in ice. They assumed it was the body of an unlucky hiker. However, the body turned out to be around 5,300 years old. By studying the body, clothing, and tools found at the scene, scientists learned  a lot about how humans lived long ago. They also discovered that the frozen body was infected with the bacteria that cause Lyme disease, making him the world's oldest known contractor of Lyme.

Discovering Lyme Disease

In 1975, the small town of Lyme, Connecticut, was the site of a medical mystery. Doctors were seeing a large number of children who had symptoms of juvenile

rheumatoid arthritis. The symptoms of this disease include fever, joint pain, and swelling. Why were so many children coming down with this unusual disease?

The children all played around wooded areas, and their symptoms started in summer. Some children had a rash, and some recalled being bit by ticks.

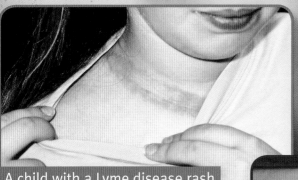
A child with a Lyme disease rash

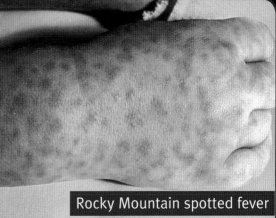
Rocky Mountain spotted fever

Two thousand miles away, Dr. Willy Burgdorfer was studying another disease, Rocky Mountain spotted fever. Burgdorfer thought it might be carried by dog ticks. When he had trouble proving this theory, a co-worker suggested he study deer ticks instead.

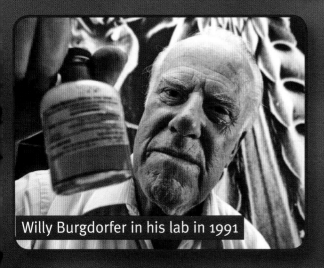
Willy Burgdorfer in his lab in 1991

Burgdorfer found strange spiral-shaped bacteria inside these tiny arachnids. Antibodies from children with the mysterious disease in Connecticut reacted to these bacteria. This proved the children's illness was caused by the tick bites. The bacteria were named *Borrelia burgdorferi* in Burgdorfer's honor. The disease itself was named for the town where it infected so many children in 1975.

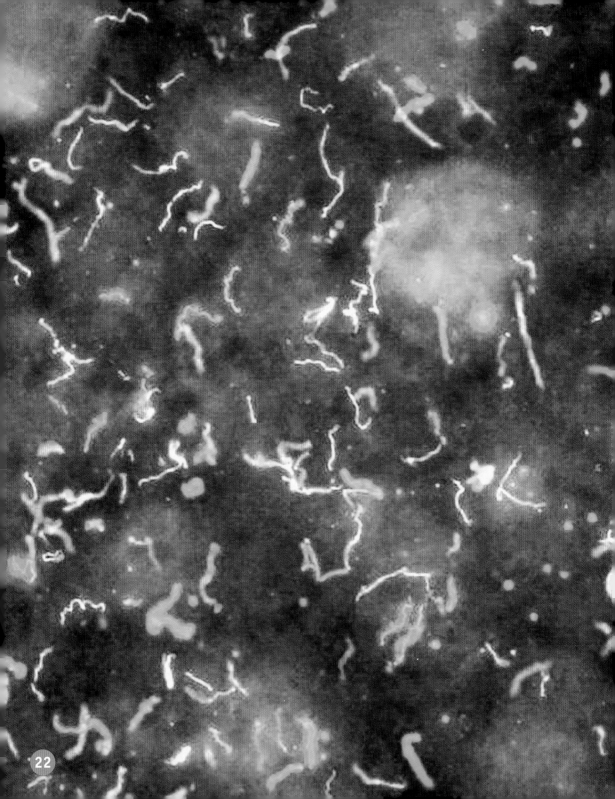

CHAPTER 3

What Is Lyme Disease?

We've already learned that you can get Lyme disease if you are bitten by a deer tick. But what exactly is it? Lyme disease is caused by bacteria that enter the body of a human **host** while a tick is attached and feeding. The bacteria move into the host's bloodstream and are carried to many different parts of the body. There, they cause varying symptoms.

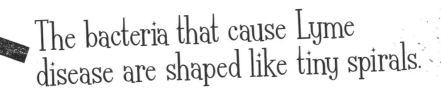

The bacteria that cause Lyme disease are shaped like tiny spirals.

A squirrel might pass Lyme bacteria to a tick, and that tick could pass the bacteria on to a human.

From One Creature to Another

Lyme disease infects animals such as mice, deer, squirrels, and opossums. When a tick feeds on an infected animal, it picks up the bacteria that cause Lyme. When that tick later bites a person, the disease can be passed on. Diseases that pass from animals to humans are called **zoonoses**. The ticks that pass the bacteria between species are not themselves sick. They are simply carriers of the disease.

How Ticks Find Their Hosts

Unlike many pests, ticks cannot jump or fly. They can only crawl onto a host as it passes by. To do that, a tick waits on a blade of grass or a leaf. It holds on with its back legs while stretching its front legs forward. When a person or animal brushes against the spot where the tick is waiting, it quickly lets go of the leaf or grass and climbs aboard.

Ticks are so small that they can climb onto a host without being noticed.

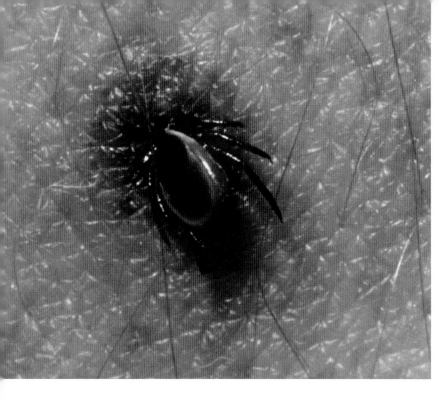

A tick bite is very small, but it can have major consequences.

Once a tick is on a host, it searches for a suitable feeding spot. Then it sinks a pair of sharp mouthparts into the host's flesh. After its mouth is attached to the host, the tick pushes in a swordlike feeding tube. It takes several days for the tick to drink a meal of blood. Spines on the tick's mouthparts keep the tick attached to the host during this time. When it is finished eating, the tick simply drops off its host.

In the first few days after a person is bitten, Lyme bacteria cause an infection near the bite. This is what sometimes causes a rash to form. Within days or weeks, the bacteria begin to move throughout the body. They cause symptoms in areas far from the original bite. More rashes, headaches, body pains, neck stiffness, and dizziness are signs that the disease is spreading.

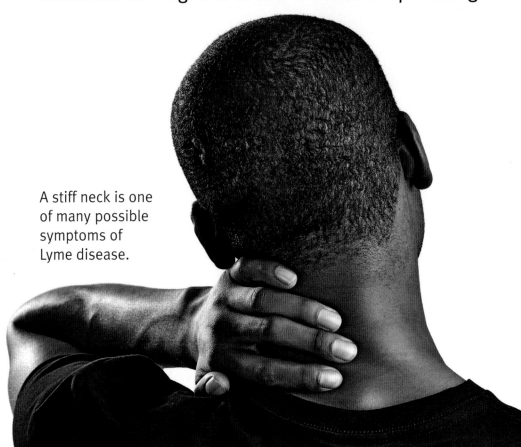

A stiff neck is one of many possible symptoms of Lyme disease.

Warm weather in the summer leads people to spend more time outside in places where ticks are found.

Some scientists think that global warming will result in more cases of Lyme disease, because ticks will be active for longer periods during the year.

A Warm Weather Disease

Many things affect a person's chances of getting a tick bite and of developing Lyme disease. One is the time of year. Ticks are most active during the spring and summer, which is when people are often outdoors. Because of this, most tick bites and Lyme disease infections occur during these months.

Where you live also plays a role. Black-legged deer ticks are the type that carry Lyme disease. They are more common in some places than others. In 2013, 14 states in the Northeast and upper Midwest regions of the United States accounted for 95 percent of reported Lyme disease cases. If you live in these areas and spend a lot of time outdoors, you will have a higher risk of catching Lyme disease.

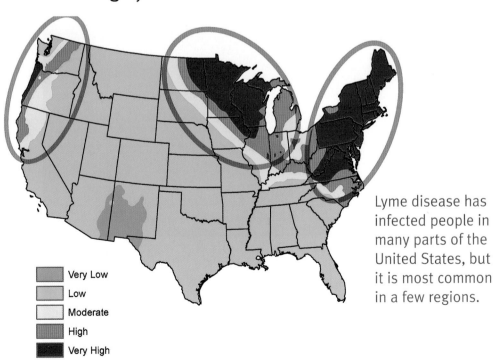

Very Low
Low
Moderate
High
Very High

Lyme disease has infected people in many parts of the United States, but it is most common in a few regions.

Many people believe that any bite from an infected tick will result in Lyme disease. This is not the case. As a tick feeds, saliva containing the Lyme bacteria enters its host's body. If the tick is attached for only a short time, little or no bacteria will be passed on. The longer an infected tick is attached, the greater the chance it will pass on Lyme disease.

Not every tick bite leads to Lyme disease.

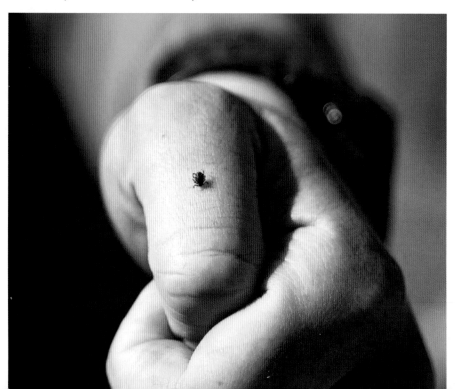

The Spread of Lyme Disease

In the 1990s, there were only about 10,000 cases of Lyme disease reported each year. But in the past few years, that number has tripled. What can explain the dramatic increase in Lyme disease? One cause is population growth. As the population increases and more people need places to live, homes are built in areas that were once wooded. This means people live closer to places where deer ticks are common.

The Centers for Disease Control and Prevention (CDC) believes that there are actually as many as 300,000 Lyme disease cases per year, with most going unreported.

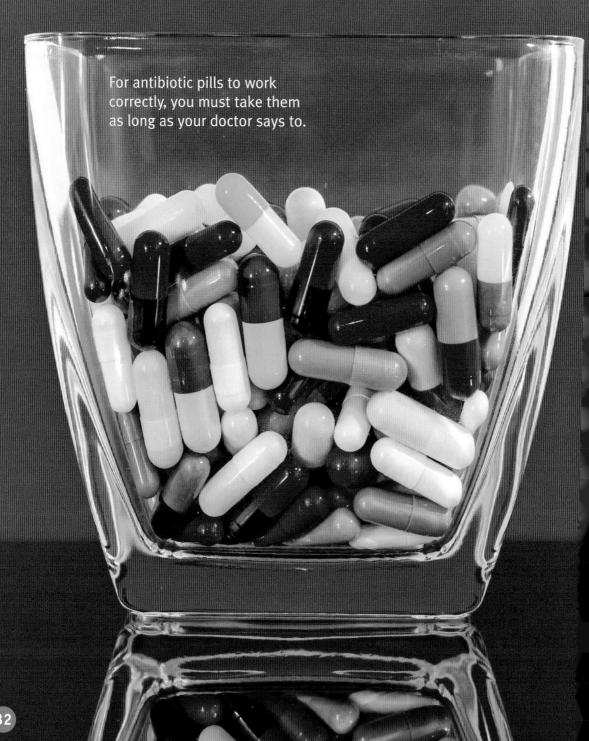

For antibiotic pills to work correctly, you must take them as long as your doctor says to.

CHAPTER 4

Treating Lyme Disease

When Lyme disease is diagnosed quickly, as Jackie's was, the treatment is usually simple and effective. Jackie's doctor prescribed **antibiotic** capsules. Jackie had to swallow them twice a day for three weeks. The antibiotics began killing the Lyme-causing bacteria in her body. After a few days on the medicine, Jackie began to feel better. After a few weeks, she was completely back to her old self.

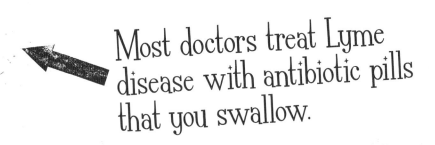

Most doctors treat Lyme disease with antibiotic pills that you swallow.

Intravenous antibiotics are often stronger than those taken as pills.

Tougher Treatments

For many other people suffering from Lyme disease, the treatment is not as simple as Jackie's. For those whose Lyme disease is diagnosed later and who have serious symptoms such as heart problems or arthritis, the doctor may prescribe intravenous antibiotics. This medicine is injected directly into the patient's bloodstream. It may be used in place of or in addition to antibiotic capsules.

For people whose Lyme disease is diagnosed later, it often takes a long time to feel better and stop having symptoms. Some people continue to have symptoms even after their treatment is complete and there is no evidence of the bacteria in their bloodstream. Doctors don't really understand what is happening in these patients.

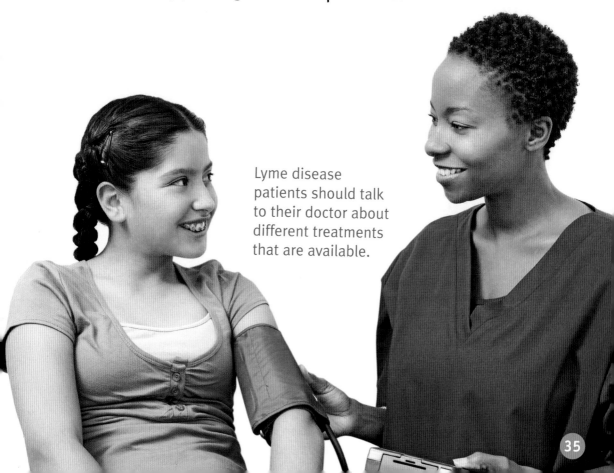

Lyme disease patients should talk to their doctor about different treatments that are available.

Chronic Lyme Disease

Some doctors believe that the Lyme-causing bacteria can trigger an autoimmune reaction. This is when a person's immune system attacks his or her own body. Doctors believe this can explain ongoing symptoms of Lyme disease. Others think Lyme bacteria stay in the patient's body and continue to cause symptoms even after treatment. These doctors use the term **"chronic** Lyme disease"** to describe patients with ongoing symptoms.

Timeline of Lyme Disease Discoveries

1975
Lyme disease breaks out among children in Lyme, Connecticut.

1981
Researchers discover the link between ticks and Lyme disease.

There is a lot of disagreement about whether chronic Lyme disease really exists. There is even more disagreement about how patients with lingering symptoms should be treated. Doctors who believe in chronic Lyme disease often prescribe antibiotics for many months or even years at a time. It is not clear whether this treatment helps relieve Lyme symptoms. The complications that come with long-term antibiotic use may create more problems than they solve.

1991
Hikers discover the 5,300-year-old frozen body of a man infected with Lyme bacteria.

2016
An estimated 300,000 new cases of Lyme disease occur in a single year.

CHAPTER 5

Preventing Lyme Disease

There's no denying that Lyme is a scary disease. Fortunately, there are many things you can do to lessen your chances of catching it. The best way to avoid a tick bite is to stay away from places where ticks live. If you are hiking, walk in the center of the trail and do not take shortcuts. Be extra careful in warmer months when ticks are most active.

Taking extra care when you spend time outdoors can help you avoid catching Lyme disease.

Protecting Yourself Against Ticks

When you do spend time outdoors, tuck long pants into your socks and wear a long-sleeved shirt. Covering your skin makes it harder for a tick to bite you. Light-colored clothing will make it easier to spot any ticks that you may pick up. Applying insect repellent to your skin will protect you for several hours of outdoor activity. You can also buy repellent to spray on your clothing.

Some places with deer ticks have signs reminding you to stay alert and helping you identify types of ticks.

If your pet was outdoors with you, check its coat and skin carefully for ticks, too.

Once you come indoors, take a shower and examine your body carefully for ticks. A small mirror can help you check places that are hard to see, such as the backs of your knees, under your arms, and in your hair. It's also important to check your clothing and backpack to make sure ticks haven't hitched a ride into your house. Put your clothes in a dryer on high heat to kill any ticks that remain.

Removing a Tick

If you find a tick attached to you, don't panic. A tick must usually be attached for 36 to 48 hours before it can pass on the Lyme bacteria. Use a pair of tweezers to grasp the tick as close to your skin as possible, then pull straight up. Do not twist the tick. This can cause the mouthparts to break off and remain in your skin.

Ticks can be removed if you use tweezers carefully.

Certain types of tweezers are made especially for removing ticks.

Clean the bite area with soapy water or rubbing alcohol. Dispose of the tick by flushing it down the toilet or sealing it in a plastic bag. Be alert for Lyme symptoms in the days and weeks after your tick bite. If you develop a rash, fever, or other flu-like symptoms, see your doctor right away. Prevention of tick bites and early treatment of symptoms are the best ways we have of fighting Lyme disease. ★

Number of confirmed and probable new cases of Lyme disease in the U.S. per year: More than 30,000

CDC estimate of the actual number of new Lyme cases each year: 300,000

Percent of people who develop a bull's-eye rash after being bitten by a Lyme-infected tick: 70–80

Time it takes for Lyme symptoms to appear following a tick bite: 3–30 days

Percent of patients who have been treated for Lyme disease but continue to have symptoms: 10–20

Number of hours a tick must be attached to its host in order to pass on Lyme-causing bacteria: 36–48

Number of U.S. states where Lyme disease has been reported: All 50

Did you find the truth?

(F) If you are bitten by a tick, you will definitely get Lyme disease.

(T) Lyme disease is much more common in some areas of the world than others.

Resources

Books

Albee, Sarah. *Bugged: How Insects Changed History*. New York: Bloomsbury USA, 2014.

Orr, Tamra B. *Antibiotics*. New York: Children's Press, 2017.

Squire, Ann O. *Flu*. New York: Children's Press, 2017.

Visit this Scholastic Web site for more information on Lyme disease:

★ www.factsfornow.scholastic.com
Enter the keywords **Lyme Disease**

Important Words

anesthetic (an-us-THET-ik) having the ability to prevent or lessen pain

antibiotic (an-ti-bye-AH-tik) a drug that kills bacteria and is used to treat infections and diseases

antibodies (AN-ti-bah-deez) substances that the blood produces to stop an infection that has entered the body

arachnids (uh-RAK-nidz) a class of animals that includes spiders, scorpions, mites, and ticks

bacteria (bak-TEER-ee-uh) microscopic, single-celled living things that exist everywhere and can be either helpful or harmful

chronic (KRAH-nik) continuing for a long time

diagnosis (dye-ugh-NOH-sis) the identification of a disease or problem from its signs or symtoms

host (HOHST) an animal or plant from which a parasite gets nutrition

immune system (i-MYOON SIS-tuhm) the bodily system that protects the body against disease and infection

parasites (PAR-uh-sites) animals or plants that live on or inside another animal or plant

zoonoses (zoh-uh-NOH-seez) diseases of animals that can spread to humans

Index

Page numbers in **bold** indicate illustrations.

About the Author

Ann O. Squire is a psychologist and an animal behaviorist. Before becoming a writer, she studied the behavior of rats, tropical fish in the Caribbean, and electric fish from central Africa. Her favorite part of being a writer is the chance to learn as much as she  can about all sorts of topics. In addition to *Lyme Disease* and books on other health topics, Dr. Squire has written about many different animals, from lemmings to leopards and cicadas to cheetahs. She lives in Asheville, North Carolina.